DAUGHTER
OF BREATH

Daughter of Breath
poems

Copyright ©2025 by Grace E. Kelley
First Published by Synthesis Press March 2025

Grace E. Kelley asserts the moral right to be identified as the author of this work.

Cover Artwork: Bethanie Pack
Cover Design: Grace E. Kelley
Author photos: Sadie Hope Seibt

First Edition
ISBN: 979-8-9866022-4-0 (Trade Paperback)

Much thanks to the following publications for publishing the original versions of the following poems:

"home(body) liturgy" (The Fallow House)
"the ascent" and "soot & soil" (The Joyful Life Magazine)

"In her brave book, *Daughter of Breath*, Grace E. Kelley bears witness not only to her own personal traumas, but to our communal ones as well. In a world where so many are devalued, Kelley finds solace and resistance in a feminist Jesus whose actual anti-empire vision has no place for hate. Reader, I urge you to draw near and listen as Kelley sings back into existence a world in which "fear is not [our] birthright--/Joy is.""

—SASHA STEENSEN, AUTHOR OF *WELL* AND *EVERYTHING AWAKE*

"Grace E. Kelley's heartfelt words give voice to harm, especially in the church, and to the healing that is already within us."

—K.J. RAMSEY, THERAPIST AND AUTHOR OF *THE BOOK OF COMMON COURAGE*

"I read (and write) a lot of poetry, and it takes something pretty special to light a fire in my soul. *Daughter of Breath* is something pretty special. These poems aren't flowery or obscure; they're poignant, piercing, and a punch in the gut. Grace E. Kelley poured her heart into these words, and there is deep healing in and between every line. What a freaking gift."

—MARLA TAVIANO, AUTHOR OF *UNBELIEVE*, *JADED*, AND *WHOLE*

"Stirring and unapologetic, this collection offers the angry a rallying cry, the broken a balm, and the overlooked an open door to belonging."

—ELIZABETH BERGET, POET AND AUTHOR OF THE POPULAR SUBSTACK *BACK OF THE FLOCK*

"Grace Kelley's words beckon and embolden readers to believe in their healing. Pain can often take our breath away, overpowering us and widening the fractures within us. But Kelley invites us to make space for our wounds, to give them oxygen, to see each jagged edge of our scars as beautiful—all in the service of casting off the voice of fear and moving toward our collective flourishing."

—JENAI AUMAN, WRITER, ARTIST, AND AUTHOR OF *OTHERED*

"To paraphrase a striking opening line from a poem in this book, Grace Kelley has, with this superb collection, claimed herself, her story, and the way in which she is, at last, allowing herself to inhabit her own life. If you have ever felt yourself to be a 'dweller on the edge', especially within the church, then these poems might just be what you have always been searching for."

"In *Daughter of Breath*, Grace E. Kelley invites us deep inside an intimate, complex, gorgeous point of view. From the raw and unfiltered angle of her pen on paper we know what it's like to have a bent (but not broken) faith, we feel the pain of being hurt by those you trusted, and we ultimately know the peace of being a beloved child of God. She fearlessly tackles patriarchy both inside and outside church walls. She sings a song of courageous womanhood and anything but frail queerness. She shows us what it's like to hurt and to heal and to love and to be gentle and to be human. This collection of poetry is breathtaking and important beyond words. The form and content were sharp when an edge was needed but soft and warm in the end. I loved, and learned from, every page."

DAUGHTER OF BREATH

Poems

Grace E. Kelley

Synthesis Press

CONTENTS

I. Man-Made Woman

II.Wind for the Wildfire

III. Visions from my Chrysalis

IV. Daughter of Breath

For my Spicy Dragon Ladies—

I never thought I deserved
to feel as free as I do
when I'm with you.

& for my daughters Ellie & Jordan—

the world will tell you
to stay quiet as mice

but

you will know
when it's time
to roar.

A NOTE TO THE READER

This book contains poems referencing religious trauma, medical gaslighting, sexual abuse, racism, queer phobia, and misogyny. None of these topics are handled in a gratuitous or graphic way, but readers with triggers should be prepared for some degree of emotional upheaval. (Let's all have a healing cry together shall we? It's good for us.)

Though this book is primarily written from the female experience with women in mind, I hope it also brings comfort and empowerment to men and non-binary folks who have had to shove down their beautifully feminine sides as "less than" as a result of our misogynistic and patriarchal culture. Many of these poems come directly from my own experiences, but not all. Some I have written as composites from the experiences of my readers, family members, friends, or from what I have seen on the news.

My prayer is that this book allows you, dear Reader, to name the aches of your own experiences of harm. Because we cannot grieve what we haven't named, and the grief must come before the healing.

Then, I pray that as you read, you'll begin to see how completely beloved you have always been. You are miraculous just for existing, and fear is not your birthright—JOY IS.

Come. Come. Let me show you.

you cannot heal

what you haven't grieved

&

you cannot grieve

what you haven't dared

to name.

DAUGHTER OF BREATH

/

"are you just trying
to make [them]
angry?"

"No.

I'm just trying
to set [her/him/them]
free."

—you are here by invitation

I. Man-Made Woman

/

words don't go void
don't return empty
handed—
but go
& find the reader—
the one sitting
in the dark.

she's shaking
& the dirt around
her ankles, the blood
between her toes
shows you
just how far she's been—
how far she still has
to go.

don't return void
words—but find her.
find her like a strong
unseen hand beneath
her chin
& point her eyes
to the heavens.

find her on the path
of her greatest weariness—
in the midst of waves
crashing overhead.

find her in the deepest
pit of darkness—
when despair
has already set in.

find her in the moment
when she's weakest—
when she's forgotten how to pray.

find her when she's stumbled
off the path altogether—

hold her hand &
lead her back
to the Way.

—the Reader & the Way

/

"only a daughter"
they spit
disappointed

irreverent of the blood
& sweat—the nine months
of labor, the beauty of a wife
giving life to another.

& we are supposed to believe
this doesn't affect us
still?

there are so few daughters in China now
so many of them murdered in the favor of sons—

even in our own country some act
as though our misogyny could be erased
in a few short generations?

how long ago was it, that a woman
could finally get a credit card without a man
to vouch for her trustworthiness?[1]

how long has it been since we
burned our bras in female liberation
declaring our own right to make a beautiful life
outside the objectification of a male gaze?

how long ago
was a woman harmed and then silenced
by a man in power?
(only yesterday—yet they demand that we forget it!)

there are still so many places
where a woman cannot inherit
I cannot stop seeing the Afghan mothers
passing their babies over the fence to the US soldiers.

---

1 Not until 1974

7

& I recently learned that a group of terrified men
tried to write my sisters out of my very own sacred text—
out of all the places they thought it might be "problematic"
for us to be

& this is why
it's important to say
that Jesus was a feminist

—the daughters are no less precious to him

/

you can blame it on the red hair
but I'm a feisty girl

& I get mad when the women I love
get pushed down.

my daughter says another girl at her school
told her that blaming patriarchy
        (for problems it has caused)
is sexist—

I know she's heard this from her father.

& if you can't see
the way misogyny
has rampantly destroyed
        the hearts
        the will
        the agency
of so many daughters—

honestly, I don't know what to tell you.
but maybe I'll just say this—

have you seen the way
they make our pants pockets?

so tiny
they are practically
imaginary—

— as if we are incapable of holding anything real

/

he called her
Mother of all
the living

but all anyone can seem to remember
is the fear-soaked bite that led
to death

—Eve too was a three-dimensional woman

/

perhaps you have forgotten
what it is to be as shining
as those 100 billion stars
in our galaxy—

I don't blame you.

the world has a way of
smothering all that brightness
which is not its own with a weighty dark—
the slightest sliver of a glow they call conceit,
as though it were for ourselves alone
that we attempt to shine!

as though the shining
of 100 billion spheres
was not a music meant
for heavens ears—

as though our voices too
weren't meant to carry
like the radio waves
into the farthest reaches of outer space—

as though our bodies
do not house the holiness
that is the very Breath
of the Divine—

(I've heard enough of little boys crying wolf
at the shadow of a tree waving gracefully
amongst moonbeams to be afraid myself
I will admit.)

but no longer—

for I am a Daughter of Breath
and fear is not my birthright—
        Joy is.

and my breath is meant for singing—
and my hips are made for dancing—
and if your skin too glows by moonlight
and if they catch you swaying with the trees,
I hope you'll join me in proclaiming once and for all
that you are not the wolf that they claim to fear—
but a Breath-Made Woman.

each inhale
and exhale
the holiest name.

—Daughter of Breath

/

I think often about the grief of Eve
giving birth to two sons only
for the jealous older to kill the younger.

I imagine she wished she herself had died
before she had seen such evil days as these
    why didn't that fruit just kill me?
I see myself in her eyes.

I imagine she thought often
about that promised son with deep hope
    who will he be?
    will he really come to crush
    the head of the serpent
    who sowed those seeds of scarcity
    in our garden of plenty?

I've heard sermons about her sin
her failures, flaws, & frailties—

—but I've never heard a sermon about Eve's grief

/

no one tells the moon
to overcome her phases—
each change a different sort of beauty
a different kind of pull
on the tides.

but I grew up hearing
that the cycles of a female body
were a liability at best
a threat
at worst.

> *don't let your feelings control you*
> *you must have mastery over your emotions*
> *the devil is in your PMS*
> *hormones are not to blame for your sin, but*
> *also*
> *they are your sin.*
> *it hurts*
> *because of Eve*
> *this is your monthly reminder.*

blaming a woman
for the pain of Women
is why it takes
10 years for the average woman
suffering monthly
from outrageous pain
to be diagnosed
with endometriosis.

is why it takes lawsuits upon
lawsuits to pursue
justice, for egg retrievals
done without proper
anesthetic.

is why when I lay
sprawled out upon

an operating table, my insides
torn apart & screaming
no one believed me
that what they called "pressure"
was actually
pain.

—misogyny runs deep in our (mis)understandings of the female
body

/

the phlebotomists say
I have good veins

all that blood pounding close
to my skin—

but I am haunted by how easily
my life could drain away

through the heartbeat
on my sleeve.

—any man with a needle could do it

/

they say it is not good
for a man to be alone

but I left you to figure it out
on your own,

all in the name
of letting you lead.

—complementarianism hurts men too

/

your credibility
    my culpability

your certainty
    my fear

your prowess
    my giftedness

your narcissism
    my joy

—things I swallowed at your command

/

they told me
my greatest gift
was something you stole
when I was seven years old

& no matter their concession
that it wasn't my fault
I still felt like
that stupid crumpled rose.

—my sexuality is not a re-gift

/

the truth is
that I was worth
less
than he was.

that's the only way
the story makes sense.

why a little girl
was forced to leave
because her abuser
was welcomed to stay.

I've observed this other times
& other places—it's hard to find
enough leaders when your pool
is 50% of the population &
when you find a man arrogant enough
you'd better hold on.

no matter that they spied
on women in the shower while on
the mission field.

no matter that they
or that their son sexually abuses children
(serially, until that ONE girl
from that ONE family
went to the cops even though
 you told them to "keep the circle small.")

no matter that they were caught grooming
a high school student for_____?
the only excuse that his wife was tired
what with all the chemotherapy.

GREAT NEWS!
this is all excusable if you have a penis.

all you have to do is say; "I'm sorry."

—you don't even have to mean it.

/

you're equal but
don't talk too much.
you're equal but
leadership requires a masculine touch.

you're equal but
this meeting is not for you.
you're equal but
isn't a smile all the payment you're due?

you're equal but
please don't ask for more.
you're equal but
it wasn't me, but God who closed that door.

you're equal but
you can't be trusted to discern.
you're equal but
your anger is cause for concern.

you're equal but
please lower your voice.
you're equal but
you only sit here by our choice.

I'm so glad you called this meeting, but please let us be clear:

if you're angry, then you're bitter
& if you're tenacious, then you're sinister
& if you disagree, then you're divisive
& if you won't just drop it, you must not be thinking of what Christ
did

& WOE TO YOU if you long to teach/ to speak /to preach about the
Goodness of Our Lord and Savior Jesus the Christ—
(just forget about that pesky woman at the well.)
woman, you're nothing but a power hungry Jezebel!

and sure maybe you would have seen the warning signs—been a little less forgiving of the flashing red lines, but that's the point isn't it? we're here to look one another in the eyes, to smile and look pretty and pretend not to see the withering soul inside (besides his sin is only a few shades darker than mine) and we said *we're sorry,* woman, why isn't that enough? forgive and forget. of what could we possibly need to repent?

so come now, dear sister, shake hands and agree!
we know how to deal with a threat to our unity.

—the dark underbelly

/

would it have been different
if a man in charge had been harmed
by a little girl

would they have taken it to the cops?
taken it to the elders?
taken it seriously?

or perhaps they shoved it under the rug
because they were afraid
that's what was happening.

a little girl coming for the reputation
of a grown ass man who did
exactly what she said he did.

—you were the monsters in my closet

/

you say to me
    "I'm sorry—
    I've changed
    the way you see him
    by telling you this—"

& I say to you:
    "NO.
    don't you be sorry.
    not for one damn minute.

he did something evil
    his evil
is what has changed
the way I see him."

—the moon is enough to illuminate this dark

/

sometimes I think
I'm just waiting for you to die

but your death
will not heal

the wounds of a life
you used to bring death
to others.

—maybe I'll wait a while longer

/

they say "you've survived
100% of your hardest days"
like bandaids on bullet wounds

but the blood won't stop flowing
& the wounds fester, gangrenous
& I don't think they'd be so bold

if they'd seen the way
I was forced to hack away
pieces of me

—so many parts of my soul left for dead

/

all I wanted was to be good.
all I wanted was to be free.

all I wanted was to be
all I was created to be.

all that I wanted was to honor Him—
to use my gifts as he saw fit,
but then you said to me
"no, no, my dear sweet sister, that just isn't it..."

I'll never forget how you asked me to speak & I was so overjoyed/ I
went overboard, my fingers clicked & clacked out all I had to say with
verses, references, main & secondary point but/ when I emailed you
for approval, I learned I'd done *too much* & all you wanted was a five
minute speech/ not for me to teach/ so I scaled it back, killed all my
darlings, *I let it go*/ only for you to use my notes for your own sermon
later/ without a single mention of me &/ don't worry I gaslit myself
into not being upset with you because/ all I wanted was for people
to be blessed/ even if that blessing could never come from me.

—oh how you used my love against me

/

"everything is sacred" she says
trailing her fingertips through calendula & rose petals
wise hands sifting
wise herbs for healing
body & soul.

in former days
wise women were just called "witches"
an easy label the small men wearing crosses
used to throw them in rivers to prove their innocence—
burning them alive if they failed to sink.

they said they were
        cleansing the town
        of unholiness;
        of evil.

but if they'd really wanted to do that
they should have thrown into the fire
        their misogyny
        their patriarchy
        their contempt for the wisdom of women
and most of all
        their envy of a power
        that did not belong to them.

why kill the wise women
gathering gifts The Breath scattered so freely
throughout this sacred world?

the real reason now please:

        *to cleanse the town
        of feminine power.*

—this is why they burned the witches

/

she told me—

"I swam like the fish
they taught me to be
but in the end
they still filleted
& roasted me."

—there is no way for a (man-made) woman to win

/

"just who
do you think
you are?"

the voice of the imposter (syndrome)
asked me every day.

I can't say when I heard it first
but it got louder the day
my beloved pastor called my writing
a "nice outlet"
as if all it could ever be was just

a little something I could do
to keep the boredom at bay
while I slowly went crazy
staring at yellow wallpaper.

yet

every day
I dared to pen audacious words
on formless pages
anyways

creating something
from nothing just like
the Breath I'm made
in the image of &

I'd think to myself

> now this...this one is garbage
> but maybe, some of it could matter?
> someday?
> somehow?
> someway?

so mild
so humble—
just like they liked me.

they told me to be
a gentle & quiet spirit
but inside I was roaring

inside I was a wild fire
consuming darkness.

the day I discovered
the double life of this beloved pastor
whose words I'd believed like gospel
I shouted at the sky
    "what the fuck
    am I supposed to do
    now?"

I'd built my life on this:
this place, this role, this carefully constructed mask
&
when it crumbled,
I felt unmoored.

    but then
like the smallest answer that led to all my biggest questions
I heard it

the Voice whispering through my tears & shouts
    "now—
    now, you *write.*"

—maybe all this time the syndrome was the imposter

/

when once again they've used
your existence
to wage their culture wars:

    your race
    your gender
    your sexuality
    your giftedness
    your struggles
    your trauma
    your aspirations

& you wonder why it feels
so icky—

maybe it's because suddenly
your desire to be seen & loved
for all the parts
that make you whole

becomes being seen for only your parts
that serve their narrative—
their pleasure.

—it's pornographic

/

it starts like this

start with a religion
full of men
afraid of women
full of themselves

gather them and stick them on boats
headed to a land they'll call "new"
surround them with Natives who worship
the Sacred Maternal & tell them
to wipe it out
because
"God is a man" & "Jesus is white"

use religion to justify
continued subjugation of the useful
& eradication of "the dangerous"

wait a few hundred years
for the Black people & Indigenous to turn the tide
the women with them calling for liberation in voices
that could no longer be denied

pretend you've fixed all the problems with
a few new laws &
a few pieces of paper.
tell "them" to stop complaining.

but know that beneath all this great nation
is the blood of the dangerous
& the sweat of the subjugated useful—

a stain that can never be scrubbed away
because it's on every rafter of the house.

—it's called trickle down oppressionomics

/

when I could only see the ways
the wrong world would wrong her—

when I could only fear that
she'd destroy herself—

when I only wondered
how I was to tame that fiery spirit—

& if she'd ever make
a "proper" wife—

I was terrified of birthing a daughter,
like I feared the match before the flame.

but I am not
any more.

—let her burn away all that should not be

II. Wind for the Wildfire

/

"you wish
you could just
open the doors,

but sometimes
they get blown off
instead."

—something Audra said to me

/

in this moment
I hate you.

because
I love you.

I
    love
        (d)
you.

/

they ask
    "how is it
    that so many abusive men
    become leaders in
    patriarchal churches?"

we tell you
    "rotting things
    smell good
    when you're
    a fly."

—but they don't believe us

/

they tried to claim me
when I did something good

"look at her, she
turned out so well!
SHE'S ONE OF OURS ALL RIGHT."

but I haven't been theirs
since the last day I looked
my abuser in the face
as he said "I'm sorry"
& the pastor smiled
like this was great success
like this would fix everything.

smiled like this boy/man
hadn't just vandalized
my body
my soul
my life
in ways I'd never be able
to entirely erase.

he smiled & it was sickly sweet
as he told us the next thing to do was
"FORGIVE & FORGET."

they forgot me alright.

until I came up
grew up
wrote poems some of them liked
(some days I hate the internet)
then they wanted to claim me
as theirs again.

"this is one of OURS!
we RAISED her! we MADE her!"

No. I'm. Fucking. Not.
& you *destroyed* me.

I stand here by the grace of God &
not the paltry "lets all get along" niceness you called grace
when you continued to let an abuser roam your halls
while I was left to flee

but the kind of grace given
to Jesus as he was tortured to death.
the kind of grace that leads an innocent to death
& resurrection.

I am alive &
I am always (becoming) free
& I have forgiven

but I will not forget &

I belong to me.

—I've worked too damn hard to let you claim any part of me

/

I wonder how many
who have preached on the value
of a faith tested by fire,

have actually stood at the edge
of what was once a flourishing field
& seen only ash
in its place.

—do you know what you are talking about?

/

the can of worms
is opened

the toothpaste is
out of the tube

the cat is out
of the bag

and how can I shove
the queerest parts of me
back in the closet again?

> there is
> no
> going
> back—

and I'm terrified
of these worms without hooks

the toothpaste mess all over
my kitchen sink

and where exactly
is this cat supposed to go now?

(as if being a christian feminist
wasn't bad enough.)

it's so disorienting—
like coming home
to all your favorite furniture
rearranged.

the family heirlooms
I used to keep in the attic
are throwing me a funeral
in my formal living room.

these hideous reminders
that my house is not only my own home,
but the home of —

every strike from
my paw-paw's unkind hands

every narcissistic snarl
insisting its own importance is the will of God

all the mother love that was lacking
the emptiness of the hearth like the emptiness of a heart

& all the seams,
the cracks,
the gaps in the walls
you keep patching
break open again
every chance they get.

my gamamma's suitcase sits
in dilapidated floral glory by the front door
and I wonder—

> would she still be
> proud of me?

or could I/*should I*
have kept all these heirlooms
locked away forever—

if only
I'd stayed
in the closet?

—it's hard coming out with generational trauma

/

I feel myself sailing downwards
hurtling towards cliffs, mountains, trees—
in a free fall I cannot stop.

my eyes sting with the rip
of the wind and I haven't breathed
easily in months but—

there is a weight
between my shoulder blades
and a cord clenched in my hand.

"dear God, this parachute is a knapsack!"
Chandler[2] proclaims & I'm right there with him
wondering

is this weight meant to save me from my crash into trees?
or is it only dead weight falling with me?

—only time will tell

/

when I fell
I hit the ground
all the tools I thought I'd used
to keep me safe
only apples & a sandwich
falling with me.

my ribs ache and
my heart feels lodged
in my throat

my bones feel crushed
and my muscles won't carry me
any further.

I am your angel
fallen from heaven
but I'm nowhere near beautiful

—I'm a bloody ruined mess

/

there was a dark august day
where I wondered—

would it hurt any worse
than it already does
to turn this knife from cutting board & zucchini
towards the heart beneath my skin?

this was not a real question,
but it was a realization.

—maybe I shouldn't chop vegetables when I feel like this

/

what if
what doesn't kill you
doesn't make you stronger?

what if it just breaks you open
until your soul
dies slowly?

—what if these fires burn the same?

/

sometimes
all I can think is
is this the desert
or the land beside the stream?

am I dying of thirst,
scraping at dry ground in fear of
scarcity?

    &
if I only looked up & around
would I find I'm mere feet
from pools of clearest
water?

—have all our false wells finally been tarred over?

/

I will move on
I will rise from this

I will open my eyes
& when my feet hit the carpet
I won't be afraid of what day brings.

I'll go on without you.
I'll step into my voice.
I'll make my choices
& do brave things
the world isn't ready for.

I thought I needed you
to hold my hand
through it all.

but as much as it hurts

—I can do this without you.

/

they told us to hide
our soft middles &
our soft hearts
& to become all angles
& edges with curves only in
the "right" places.

why is 'right' only
what the male gaze deems
desirable?

can't my soft middle
be the sign of beauty?
my soft heart on my sleeve
the proof—

that life giving and life taking
are opposites &
I know my gaze is generous,
can the same be said of you?

don't strip me of my clothes
or my dignity!
I give no consent for the way your eyes
graze my lines
parsing the parts & pieces of me
for your pleasure.

I do not exist to temper your curiosity
or sate your carnal pleasure—
nor did I come here
or talk like this
or dress this way
or walk with this swish to my hips
in order to beg for this from *you.*

I AM ONE WHOLE WOMAN,

& I am round and soft,
full of life and that Power
in my confident step—
the swing of my hips,
has nothing to do
with *you.*

I am not your heaven,
　　nor the temptress that will lure you to hell.

but I am a Daughter of Breath—

　　AND I HAVE WORK TO DO.

—I am more than the men who see me

/

if the white men
were dying
of preventable _____ complications

wouldn't they
say something?

—on the maternal health crisis in the United States of America

/

on days when I wake up
to murder in the news,

I open the curtains
& let in the light.

I kiss the toddlers on their foreheads
& I teach them to be kind.

I take ripe tomatoes
& gently peel their skins,
mixing them with jalapeños & onions,
spices & vinegar;
a salsa we'll enjoy all winter long.

& I say a prayer.
& I shed some tears.

& I write this poem.

what else can I do
in the face of heinous evil?

but affirm
the beauty of life
& let in the light.

—I am small, but I am not powerless

/

if you only care about the unborn as long as they don't cost you anything,
please turn in your pro-life card.

if you only care about the babies if they're white like you or their mothers & fathers talk like you, dress like you & worship like you,
please turn in your pro-life card.

if the Brown babies burning in Palestine don't sour your stomach for days on end,
if the Black boys shot by police don't follow you like haunted heralds of injustice,
please turn in your pro-life card.

if you don't know/care that the maternal mortality rate in the United States is 3X higher among Black mothers because of racial bias in medicine—

if you aren't worried about the mothers in Texas bleeding out in the hospital parking lots because they can no longer access reproductive care—

meanwhile you continue to fight for that "second amendment right" to keep open access to deadly weapons without the benefit of common sense protections leaving our children trapped & defenseless —

please turn in your pro-life card.

it was the same in the pandemic you know?
when people who claimed to protect life held signs that read

    SACRIFICE THE WEAK

& if you don't know anyone that falls in the "weak" category
the "othered" category,
the "least of these" category that Jesus held in such a tight embrace
then—

maybe stop pretending that this is about God & just admit
this is about scarcity
about fear
about hate.

if immigrant lives don't count just
turn it in now.

if disabled lives don't count just
turn it in now.

if queer lives don't count just
turn it in now.

if trans lives don't count just
turn it in now.

don't say; "this is war/ this is our country/ our religion/ our world
& these things (people) are just collateral damage, their losses 'a
fact of life' for the rest of us to 'get over.' you never know just how
expensive the bill is when you are not being asked to pay it & the
least you could do is listen to the least of us when we're telling you
that if you want us to believe you are pro-life you need to be pro-
all-life & it doesn't take a bleeding heart liberal to see the hypocrisy.

if you're so bent on your declaration of "loving life"/ protecting hate
that you can't see how these things can possible relate
then I'm sorry to tell you, but it's time.

go ahead.
I'll wait.

—please turn in your pro-life card

/

there is such a fear
in being seen as I
(actually) am

    but also—

such hope.

—I'm just a woman looking for water

/

she said to me;

"show me your worst--
let the [wounded] animal of your soul
        free
from her cage.

[your rage
does not frighten
me."]

but I said to her;

"how can that be true
        for you
when it isn't even true
for me?"

and we sat in silence
until she knew
I knew
she meant it.

and to You I say:

"FIND THIS!
there is a friend
who won't abandon
you[r
        broken parts]

even though
you long ago
abandoned [them]
yourself."

—find this

/

you roll in dark & wild
& mystery is in your molecules.

your laugh like thunder
makes me shake with delight.

your strong heart broken
& mended, before I'd ever stood
beneath your shade.

& what I need you to know is—

I am a woman
who has lost faith in women
        time and time again—

but when I stand on mountain tops alone
& you rush in with the speed of a storm-wind
& I am caught in a deluge of being wanted
as I actually am—
sometimes the joy almost hurts
& sometimes the happiness makes me fear.

I am exposed on this hillside
& you could strike me if you wished—
        but you don't.

instead, your rain soaks through
my apron & all these dangling strings,
cooling my sunburned face as I lift my gaze
to thank the Storm-Wind that blew you my way
one fateful august day.

can you see it?

you are more than some pitiful
puff of cloud without form or substance—
        YOU ARE A STORM BREWING
& the deadwood on the hillsides is aching
for the renewal that only fire can bring.
& my heart is aching to dance
in a sudden summer rain.

I watch you roll in dark & wild,
with mystery in your molecules,
& I know your strong heart broken & mended
has begun to mend the tears in mine.

—I thank the Storm-Wind that brought You to Me

I.

could I have known then
what I know now?

her tiny frame, covered in soot
blue eyes howling from beneath
red lids & dark lashes

tiny hands clasped on knees
when they ought to be fighting—
fighting their way out

the house is burning down.

II.

I was the same—
once.
slim, wide eyed
less feisty perhaps but fierce.
we have the same lips
my mother once told me.

but I can't know any of this yet;

for I am just a girl &
 impossibly—so is she.

III.

smoke & heat pressed in
pressed down, held me
against my will.

my ragged body
battered & burned
my dress—torn.

blind—longing I searched
for the door, but a beam
nearly fell on me

nearly crushed me.
or at least
what was left—

when the smoke had had his way.

IV.

but blind eyes see
through words of hope
all things for the good

like the crackle of a bullhorn
like the crack of cold air—
from a door suddenly ajar?

—I ran.

V.

back. back. back
through the flames
to the girl with eyes of bluest pain

could I have known?
would it have been too much—
or more than enough?

this is a house without a clock.

VI.

she looks at me in relief,
like she knows something

I do not.

I take her hand in my
 only slightly larger one.
we feel the cool air move

closer to our upturned faces,
with a heave, I shove at the open crack
of the door

—we break free.

VII.

it's only in the aftermath,
watching the house burn down
that I know her.

her face as familiar
as her smell in those early days
of late night feedings &
early morning mercies.

I am no longer a child—I am grown
& the fire was not just mine,
it was hers.

VIII.

she is every age here,
as am I.
existent in some form aside from those
so tied with time.

old or young,
she's mine. where we sit by the stream
& wash soot from our bodies,

I know now that I have bathed her
a thousand times.

IX.

we don the clean dresses
someone had left
lying on the bank.

& I know which Someone
left them instinctually;
the Voice from the bullhorn,

the Voice
that changed everything—

all things for the good.

X.

when the house has burned
all down to ashes
this is what I intend:

that we will turn over all this soot & soil—
& we will plant a garden.

could I have known then
what I know now?

that I would walk through fire
for that girl,

& I already did.

—soot & soil

/

I threw us
into another tornado
or maybe
it was a hurricane

or perhaps a maelstrom
we'd been circling
for a long, long, time.

I didn't mean to hurt you.
but I did.

I know it hurt to know
I hadn't been completely honest
(I hadn't been honest with myself)

& I know you're worried
I can't love you like I did
before,

but it's not that.
only—
        this
        is
        Who
        I
        Am.

(now) &

who I have always been
beneath the layers of niceties & propriety
& all the things the (christian?) world
told me to be or not to be.

& I know that must be hard to hear.

& you aren't sure how to tell anymore
if the ground beneath you is solid
or a swirling vortex of black
leading to the bottom of the sea.

but what I'll throw out to you like a buoy
or a life preserver is that
    you are the partner
    I choose for my life.
&
    I'm right here.

that hasn't changed.

hold on.
just hold on
a little longer.

this maelstrom
cannot last
forever.

—just hold on

/

what if
I'm only a mess
right now?

what if this
is not
forever?

what if I'm the caterpillar
wound up in a chrysalis
my outsides disappearing &
all that I once thought of as 'me'
has been liquified.

how vulnerable!

I could be squashed this very minute
& no one would even be able to identify
what I once was.

but given time—

once my cells have rearranged
& organized themselves anew—

once I can fill my wings with blood,
until the fragile becomes firm—

then I'll stretch out in the sun until
all that was unsightly & grotesque moments ago

has now become the thing
that makes me capable
of flight.

—metamorphosis has always been messy

III. Visions from my Chrysalis

/

I have been furthest
from delighted
or delightful.

weights have weighed
me down like rocks
in the poetess' pockets
dragging me down
to the bottom of the sea.

& how can I see
clearly? with all
these fathoms of seas
above me?

the light filters down
to my upturned eyes
but it only makes me
envy those who ride
the waves.

I was there once;
fighting for my life
with each roiling swell
trying to keep my head
above water.

it was then that you
lifted me —
to walk like Peter
among the waves.

but now, the white caps
have pummeled me
one too many times
& my pockets are lined
with heavy stones
& I can't see you
    —anywhere.

& if the joy
of the Lord is strength
well—no wonder
I am so exhausted.

in despair I turn my eyes
from the light, from my envy
of those who walk on water—

but it's then that I see you.

drawing near & nearer
reaching around me
your strong arms
taking the rocks
from this poetess' pockets
& taking my hand—

& oh the delight!
you are not where I saw you last—

but you are where I am.

no depth too deep for you.
no weight too great
for your strong shoulders.

my pockets emptied
you take my hand—
but you don't drag me along
at some efficient clip.

instead you hold me steady
as the water lets us
slowly ascend.

—the ascent

/

they are laughing when I ask them;
"tell me what is your favorite story
of Jesus' interaction with a woman?"

they are quiet at the table where we've feasted
on fresh veggies, hummus, muffins, & popcorn
camaraderie turned to an aching silence.

I say again; "not the way they taught us to see,
not the way the stories were preached,
just *the way He treated women*.

remember how;

Martha was angry that Mary wouldn't help & / Jesus issued an
invitation for her to sit as well?/ remember how he saw the woman
at the well/ & spoke to her (though she was a Samaritan & even
among them had been ostracized?) / she was the first one he told
that he was Messiah / remember how he saved the life/ of the
woman brought before him in the very act of adultery/ telling the
men who had gathered that only the sinless/ could cast a stone at
her/ & remember how he didn't chide Mary when she accused him/
of letting Lazarus die? he only held her gaze &/ let his own tears
flow?/ before bringing her brother back to life/ & remember how he
hugged Mary Magdalene in the garden outside the tomb / knowing
she needed more than seeing but also feeling in her body / that this
man she'd followed to the ends of the earth / had stood sentry by
& watched die/ was actually alive / & remember how she was the
first he entrusted with the message *He is Risen*. / & every easter
liturgy since is a repetition of the words of a woman / & remember
the woman who bled / the woman with the demons / the woman
with the cripple spine / the little girl who was dead/ remember
how many times he called DAUGHTER / someone the religious had
called CURSED / how many times he looked into the eyes / of those
the world had long cast aside?"

their eyes lift in
heavy quiet—
different this time.

75

it's on their faces
its in the lines of their frames
the words;

I've never heard it told
like that before.

—he's still there between the words of broken men

I

look there!
through the trees
Glory's overshadowing
covers those living
under the shadow of death—
& the One who conceived
constellations & comets—
giving them birth with a shout of joy
is himself conceived & formed
in a womb he made out of dust.

see now!
he who labored to lay low
ocean floors & raise up horizons
lay low in the pelvis of a woman
laboring long amongst the ewes
bleating with their newborn lambs
these other mothers of sacrifice.

hear how her sighs
signaled the shattering of sorrows
as he who was
emerged at last—
in water, blood & vernix
swirling like the milky way
Mary's tears of relief
a prophecy of longing & of joy.

listen!
his first cry signaled it was safe
to hope again, as he lay
in a feeding trough,
the cut grass beneath him
smelling of both life & death—
of a sacramental feast.
like the bread of life rising
from grains crushed to dust—
like the stars long dead
still shouting in the silence
            "GLORIA! he's here!"

you could hear them for miles!
the great hosts of heaven
belting with a boom like thunder
        "GLORIA! he's here!"

                    how terrifying!
these songs of glory & peace
must have sounded to these
least of these shepherds stood aghast
until at last, they too saw the babe
wrapped in swaddles as foretold.
                    the holiest in the lowliest—
and you could see it
in their awestruck faces
                    this story is too strange

to be a lie—
                    who could conceive it?

watch them bolt through city streets,
their feet pounding out
the sound of joy pouring out
of their dry lips
        "GLORIA! —he's here!"
who could conceive?
of God wrapped in fragile flesh—
        "GLORIA!
        he's here

                    —at last."

—Glory's Overshadowing

/

I sat there on the porch steps
smelling warm spring petrichor
staring up at points of effervescent light,
thinking of how the chance of lightning
is really only a matter of clouds
& static

& time.

my heart was rent,
one half sitting fleshy pink
in my upturned palms
like a prayer—

the other half (belonging to the woman
I had always believed myself to be)
lay like a stone in my throat
suffocating.

"do You love me—
    still?

& is it
    in spite of...
OR (could it be?)
    because of...

is this piece of me
this lump of pink in my upturned palms—

    perversion to abhor
or
    creation to adore?"

I held the questions as I held my heart
& all the lesson I'd been taught
about how I ought to be
& the terrifying fear that it is
the wide road to hell for me
flew out from beneath my feet
at the words You spoke to me;

"see! there is a roadmap in the velvet black
a way still in the wilderness
& the stars still lead the way
to this Truth:
that though you are small you are also
        significant—
a sign
a point
of effervescent light
in the darkest night

&

        you
        are
(still)
        MINE."

/

those who said
they would help
have only hurt me
more.

the blood
won't stop
coming & all
these wounds
refuse to be
bound.

but I heard a rumor
yesterday—

they say:
a man—
a prophet—
a healer—
has come.

in the crowd
I hide my face
behind my shawl.

I don't belong here.

all who touch me
are unclean &
in this crowd
I could pollute
dozens—yet do I really
seek to touch *him?*

not him
I say to myself
just his hem—

after all this time
walking alone
perhaps I could be
a mother—
a friend—

a daughter—
again.

my fingers
graze fabric & I feel
the Power working.

my body feels
more whole
than it has in
twelve long years,
but with the joy comes
a lightning flash
of terror.

what have I done?

but before I can slip
away anonymous &
unnamed his eyes
turn toward me.

he asks
"who touched me?"
& I, shaking admit
"it was me."

I thought
he would
chastise me
for making him
unclean—

instead I feel
his hand beneath
my chin, lifting
my eyes to his gaze
& I hear the words;
"Daughter, your faith
has made you whole."

& isn't that
what faith is meant
to do?

his dark eyes sparkle
with joy & with mischief
healing parts of me
I didn't know
were broken.

—just his hem

/

I want to ask her
"do you feel safe?"

does your breath slow
does your heart rest
can you let the soft animal
Mary Oliver spoke of love
what it loves
without fear?

can you eat your favorite foods
without judgment?

can you kiss the person
you love in public
without harassment?

can you close your door
against the world at night
& sleep secure
that you are not about to be
the next victim
on the news?

if the answer is yes, then
REJOICE!

but
if the answer is no then
sit with the places and spaces that make you say
No
& listen—
& I will listen too.

what choices do you have?
if any—&

how do you go on
while honoring
that you have every right
to feel safe

but don't?

—it's okay. you can tell me your whole truth.

/

I know
your heart
is full of anguish
& longing—

     mine is too.

how I have longed
to gather you
beneath my plumage;
as a mother hen
gathers her vulnerable
chicks—shielding them
from all that would seek
to do them harm.

I would treat
your wounds
with the balm
of my presence &
cure your sorrow
with the sound
of my laughter.

     oh if you only knew
     how I delight
     in you!

but you have been
wayward sons & daughters—
Jerusalem the Holy City
slaughters the prophets
& those who are sent
to seek and save it.

     yet I would gather you
     even still;

—children who cannot
believe a promise

only because it
isn't the way
you imagined it.

—children who cannot
believe my words
because your eyes
have yet to see
them come true.

—but it was for this reason Beloved, that I have come.

/

I was in the back
of the synagogue
like I always was—

my back hunched
my neck straining
he called out to me—
        "Woman you are Free!"
he threaded his way
through the crowd to me

& as he laid his rough hands
on my slumped shoulders
they rose to their proper place.
I found to my surprise & delight,
I could look straight into the face
of this Rabbi— see the smile behind
his spotty reputation for heresy & healing.

I did not break his gaze
at the rustle of angry men behind him,

but then I realized they were speaking to me.
        "you shouldn't have come
        today for healing!
        it's the Sabbath!"

& the gentle face before me
looked for a moment grief stricken
then all at once,
full of rage.

        "You hypocrites!"
he turned to shout,
his kind hand still gentle on my
newly healed shoulder.

"hasn't she waited long enough?/ don't you each day/ (even on the
Sabbath)/ set free your ox or donkey/ & bring it to water? / because
it is yours & you care for it?/ well, this Daughter of Abraham is
mine./ & today is the day/ for her to be set free."

now the synagogue leader's face turned red &
he opened his mouth to speak,
but no words came.

yet all the people rejoiced with me.

— everything my sisters told me about this carpenter was true

/

maybe just this once
I'll refuse to read the recipe
before I begin

may be I'll go in blind as you
always did and start hacking
my way through vegetables

step
   by
     step
        by
          step

unsure what I'm making
unsure of how this
will all turn out

—just as I've always been because of you.

/

Jesus has always
aligned himself
with the women
at risk of being stoned.

the sex workers &
the women caught
in the throes of illicit
passion.

the 'sinful' woman
pouring a dowry's
worth of perfume
on his feet.

his own unwed
mother.

I realize that this too
may make you angry

may make your palms ache
where you clench rock & stone.

—are you ready now to walk away?

/

here lies
grace she
was every
thing she
was suppo
sed to be

& nothing
that she
wasn't.

but she got tired of being good enough/ of being only the "right"
kind of visible/ she was self-less until her self/ wasted away to
nothing &/ then she wondered where the light in her eyes had
gone? &
she got
tired of
pretend
ing to be
"normal"
helpful
low-main
tenance or
straight

(as if heter
osexuality
is the para
gon of virt
ue)so she'll
tell you she
's a feminist
& she's bi
sexual &

maybe to you that means she is no longer the ideal christian woman
& maybe no one /will praise her or call her blessed/ but she will live
free now & Jesus loves her this she knows & wasn't that the point of
grace to begin?

—the point of grace

/

did you know that
every time a queer kid
sees a rainbow

it makes them think
that maybe God
actually loves them?

does that make you angry?

as if God isn't big enough to hold all
the fractals & facets of every rainbow
& rainbow-colored child

—even as he's holding you

/

birds sang merry & defiant
while tears of rage & grief
poured themselves down Mary's face
where she sat by the window
in the upper room,
waiting
for night to fall.

> "I need to prepare the spices
> his body needs to be attended to,
> even if he is in that borrowed tomb.
> after all he did for us in life
> it's the least that I can do."

but Sabbath had stopped her anxious work
for the only man who'd ever truly seen her,
so she'd been sitting still & silent
by the window all morning,
listening to birdsong
as if the little creatures were saying;

> *all shall be well*
> *and all shall be well*
> *and all manner of thing shall be well.*[3]

the next day arrived, in much the same way.
all the springtime chirping & warm whistles
serenaded Mary Magdalene & her friends along
the rocky roads & through the dark garden paths—

her heart was a stone in her chest as she walked in silence,
the other women beside her. But, she couldn't help but wonder
just for a moment,
if perhaps these little birds knew something
she'd forgot.

> "what was it he used to say
>   about the sparrows?"

she asked the other Mary suddenly.
her throat was tight as she tried to remember
tried to see his face in her mind's eye,
without that cruel crown of thorns
without the sky going dark as her heart as he died.

---

3 a quote from Julian of Norwich   93

suddenly, the ground began to shake
& terror filled her heart as she ran the last few steps
to that borrowed tomb, the spices in the satchel at her waist
her only weapon against death.

to her horror, the stone was rolled away
the tomb—silent & empty.
she stumbled out into the light of morning
birds still singing as she reeled

> *where have they taken him?*
> *where have they taken him?*
> *how could they do this to me?*

a voice behind her
> "Woman, why are you crying?
> who is it that you are seeking?"

she thought maybe his steps belonged
to the man in charge of tending to this garden
& maybe the rich man had changed him mind
about letting a crucified heretic use his tomb.
> "Sir, if you've carried him away,
> just tell me where you've put him
> & I will take care of him."

but then he said;
> "Mary—"
& she would know that Voice anywhere.
> "Teacher!"
she cried, throwing her arms around his neck
laughing into his chest as he told her,
> "you can hold on for a moment,
> but not forever, not yet.
> there is much to be done
> Daughter—in the meantime,
> go & tell my brothers
> that I am ascending to our Father,
> yours & mine."

—& all shall be well even after the darkest night

/

on days when she needs reminding
that god is love and love is for her

Miranda takes a walk & finds
hearts made of stone or twig or leaf

Laura gazes into golden retriever eyes & basks
in the joy of being cherished as she is

& Sarah watches the clouds
& Audra studies the stars

& Liezel takes a walk
& Sadie reads one of Liezel's poems[4]

&

on the day I come out to my parents
the rain sweeps in wild & holy
        (it always was a gift of The Breath to me)
& when it leaves I'm left in
double rainbow light.

—drunk on the reminder that I've been loved all along

IV. Daughter of Breath

/

I know you have sometimes wished
to be smaller

to tuck yourself
in tidy origami folds

so you could fit *just so*
inside their front breast pocket

but you have always been more
than a colorful scrap of satin &
I'm here to tell you

—that is no life for you.

/

as a child she'd always listened
to the Voice beneath her skin—
the wisdom held within her
Breath-Given intuition.

when she grew up she met
some christians who had a name
for what that was—"the Holy Spirit"
they called it, "a gift!" they said

(& it was)

that is until the Voice spoke truths
they didn't like—
until it had her speaking up,
when things in church weren't right.

they forced her out in the end
& now she's back from whence she came
only now she isn't sure what to trust
now that they gave her Voice their name.

—how easily they blaspheme the Spirit of the Breath

/

I am a champagne bottle
being shaken

there is a pressure building
that I cannot tamp down.

I fear the explosion
even as I seek it like release—

what will come next?

who will celebrate & who will only
complain about the mess?

either way
Jesus is sitting next to me

—a glass in his hand

/

I no longer listen
to any voice
that tells me
to silence
my own.

—I know who I am

/

you have forgotten perhaps—
but if you were to remember?

then perhaps you might see
how your fingertips trail
with flower petal smoothness
over all that is rough hewn and raggedly wounded?

perhaps you would see
that you were breathed into
for the very joy
of your existence

you are the answer
to the "help wanted" ad

& it's not a small or paltry thing
to bring powerful aid.

but we are a culture that thinks too little
of those who help.

but the sun
is a help & so is
the rain
& the wind
strengthens the root of the trees
(the biodome showed us they cannot
stand without it)

so who are they to say
that you are supplemental
or tertiary
or any of that cockamamie bullshit?

you are not a helpful table
at the back of a book—
you are as necessary as the binding,
the ink, the words—

it's just not a book
without you.

—so God made a Woman

/

"thank you
for asking
for what you
need."

—things I say to my children (that I also need to hear)

/

I wish I could hold you
the day more children die
on the news

I know how it kills you
to not be able to prevent this evil

for all your perceived power
you feel powerless

but you are not.

you can still do your work
& your work matters.

— believe me, you're making a difference

/

my father says
it's in my blood &
my Gamama had it.

she taught a bible study for 10 years
before the new pastor told her
"it's not your place."

    it was the greatest heartbreak of her life
my father tells me.

my Grandma too
traveled the world to share the news
only to be shoved in the children ministry box
upon her return to the United States.

(& maybe that's the box she really wanted to be in,
& the children were certainly worth
her passion & conviction
 but—I long to ask her;
    is that what you really wanted?
    or only what our society deemed appropriate?)

this desire to speak
about the good
the beautiful
& the true—

it has always been there
simmering beneath the surface
boiling its way through my veins.

I spent so long contorting myself for their boxes
I made myself
so
so
quiet &
small

because they convinced me it was God's will
& I love god.
& also—it was what I needed to believe
to belong.

(this part feels ugly & embarrassing
but it is true.)

conformity to strict gender roles has become irrefutable
gospel truth
to so many[5]

three years it's been since
I left that place.

not long.

but long enough for the quiet in my own soul
to sweep away the cob webs of that siren song
of (perceived) safety & (conditional) belonging.

instead—
the song of my blood, a drum beat in my chest
& the Voice, a cauterizing whisper in my ear—

Speak!

—*tell them how much I love them.*

---

5 Read Beth Allison Barr's book *The Making of Biblical Womanhood* for in-depth historical
analysis of how this came to be.

/

when my bare feet trace the laminate path
between my whistling copper kettle,
the cupboard where I keep my tea,
and wherever I left my tea pot last;
    I know that I am home.

when I smell onions sweetening
themselves in melted butter
in my dutch oven red-as-candied-apples,
the wedding present I didn't know I needed;
    I know that I am home.

when I sit in my comfortably worn
floral patterned wing chair, a book
in one hand, a child in the other,
a shabby quilt over us both;
    I know that I am home.

when I lie down beside you
not facing you exactly, but stretching
my calf, my ankle, my toes out behind me
to make a point of contact with you;
    I know that I am home.

here at home
when the music plays
I know it's safe to let my thighs shake.
I'm safe to spin on the toes of my holey socks
and leap with imagined grace.
    don't tell me
    if you saw me
    through the window.
    I do not want to know.

here at last
I can turn on the tap—
I can open my mouth wide,
tilt my head to the side
and drink deep of the cool freshness.
    this is my
    (home)body
    liturgy.

my home is hallowed
and hollowed—
filled to overflowing with
cups of tea or maybe
bowls of soup;
fitting, filling, warming
my ice cold hands
    —*just so.*

and people!
lots of people
each an aching beauty—
the words between us
rising as an offering
    as the steam
    from my cup rises
    to greet the sun.

—(home)body liturgy

/

I'm ready for the dirty feet of summer
and the slam of the screen door
as little feet abandon civility
for the wildness of a mud pie feast.

I'm ready for the smell of wet earth
and storm clouds and fresh hay—
and for the song of the frogs
to sing us to sleep.

I'm read to sit in the shade
of my front porch with the man I love—
a glass of whiskey lemonade in each
of our garden worn hands.

I'm ready to sing/shout out
the rolled down car windows
like I believe that freedom is a gift
meant for me.

I'm ready to throw open curtains
at 5:45 am to watch the sunrise
from the comfort of my downy bed
with a cup of steaming tea.

here is what I need you to know, because
maybe you need to hear this too—

not all my days are an iced coffee Sunday where I remember
that rest does not have to be earned
and neither does joy.

but for today,
I step out into the day and open up my palms
ready to receive them both.

—for today

/

today the darkness was nipping
at my bare heels

so I showed my twin toddlers
how to pickup perfectly
sun-ripened tomatoes for soup.
    gently—
I said,
    like this.

while I diced the small garden onions
my tears fell on the cutting board
& my son asked me,
    why you crying mama?
& I said,
    it's just the onions baby.
& kissed the soft hair of his head.

but I let my prayers rise like steam,
from the frozen pesto cubes I added for flavor.
    don't touch
I tell my daughter,
    it's hot.
she heeded me,
though she doesn't always.

I too am still learning to listen
& hear, the gentle Voice
instructing me in what is mine to do,
& what isn't—especially on the darker days.

& there in my kitchen I heard it,
like a drum beat I can live my life to:
    act justly
    love mercy
    walk humbly.

—sometimes the sun-ripened moments are sermon enough

/

"I'm cold"
she says—
her first words of the day
reflecting only need.

so I open up the blanket on my lap
& wrap her in warmth
her soft hair tickles my chin in the dawn light.

& all I want to say to you
are the words I hear in my head
with the weight of my daughter in my lap—

your neediness
is not
to be
despised.

—remember scarcity was the first lie we are faulted with believing

/

I say I believe
in a non-binary God
& I realize this may come as a great shock

& yet its all there
even in the ancient texts
you worship

>how God the Breath
>made male | female
>in their image

>the pronoun used for YHWH
>neither masculine nor feminine
>(english is to blame for this mis-
>understanding)

>the triune three persons
>both a plural &
>a beautiful ONE
>a unity

what holds us together? | what keeps us safe |
& what is allowed to be beautiful?

God is still to say on those ones
don't get me wrong. But what
s/he/they speak to me seems very different
than what you say
s/he/they speak to you.
(Is your blood boiling at my use of pronouns?)

in 2,000 years will the translators know the difference
between a "butt dial" and a "booty call"?
(I saw this on the internet.)

was sodom destroyed
for homosexuality?
or rape?

which is worse to you?
(please you really don't need to answer that.)

and ADAM only means HUMAN
& what if our humanity
has always mattered more
than our sexuality or complexities
in our gender identity?

what if the non-binary beloveds
image our supra-sexual god
in a unique way—

what if the church
is missing out?

the fluidity of god
the Breath
the maker of every good
and perfect thing

S/he/they need no containing
& I'd like to point out that
for all you know Jesus was as queer as me.
noticing the beauty of all
is not sin;

failing to see
a created being's beauty
as one made in the imago dei
on the other hand—

now that is.

—enby God

/

maybe it's like kintsugi—
woven through my cracks
a golden thread holding all
that trauma tried to break.

—is this what they mean by queer joy?

/

sometimes
I walk around my house
looking for poems.

I can always find one—
if I have eyes to see.

the dents in the walls
where you threw your keys
the day your cousin died.

the place Jordan scrawled blue
across my white cabinets
leaving her mark upon our world.

what kind of poem
will I write today?

will I tell the story of the scar on my chin—
of how I fell when he chased me
of how I lay disgusted & afraid in the dark.

or will it be a poem
about the dust dancing joyful
in the autumn light through my dirty windows?

life holds so much—
but it takes freedom to see it
to name it.

—I wish this freedom for you too

/

you have never met
a mortal woman.
all of us are sparkling
nebulae, the birth places of stars.

our bones hold building blocks &
our hips cradle worlds &
our lips speak light
into the darkest parts of space.

it's 2024 and they cannot identify the purpose
of every atom of our milk—but they know now
there probably is one.
(they've learned to trust that much.)

& never forget the magic of baby backwash
how our breasts take in infant saliva
detecting illness, adding antibodies
to make the child well.

my body parts—
I once thought of as mere vacancy
        emptiness
        lack.
I'd look to the boys and hear
        "now this child has something
        you do not"

(and wouldn't Freud have been tickled pink—)

but this is not what I am—
nor am I limited to the miracles my body can create
(I have made five of these, and I love them feverishly,
but this too is not all of me)

for I am in everything
        Imago Dei
conduit & conductor
created & creative

& what you need to know about nebulae is
that the gas between the galaxies is not empty air
        but space.

—the infinities I would create with a bit of earth/space/time

/

see here?
these burning coals
these embers are only a breath away
from leaping again into flame

though today
it feels impossible
& today
I know you are so
fucking
tired.

I know they've stepped on you
& doused you with water until you screamed
& scattered you away from your sisters
but I'm begging you now—

don't let the fire die

the ember you hold within
is only waiting
to break open again & burn—
tomorrow maybe

& even now
it still warms me
when I press my palms close
to your beating heart

I can control so very little

but I can keep the bodies close to mine warm
& I can invite others into the circle
& I can gather the embers from where they've been scattered
beat the drum & dance & sing aloud until
all of us are a glowing, burning, bonfire—

burning down the palaces
where they pretend to be kings.

—don't let the fire die

A NOTE AFTERWARDS

Dearest Reader,

If you are like so many of us, you may have found parts of this work to be pretty activating and potentially triggering. I hope you know you are not alone in this, and if you find yourself feeling restless upon finishing this work, I have a few suggestions for you to help move some of those feelings out of your body.

1. Somatic movement. If you're feeling numb or stuck, lace up your shoes and take a walk. Allow the feelings to flow through your body. It can be overwhelming, but I promise you, the feelings will dissipate after you've allowed them the space to move through you.

2. Scream/sing your favorite feminist rage songs while you clean your house. (This works especially well while vacuuming, but I also love to do it while scrubbing my kitchen sink.) Don't be surprised when the tears come. Sadness often masquerades as anger.

3. Share the poems that were particularly meaningful to you with a friend, or read this book with a group. (Check out my website gracekelleywrites.com for a free book club discussion guide!) I know from experience that connections built around shared words can be one meaningful way to build a real life community that will encourage and uplift you as you reclaim your identity as a Daughter of Breath.

4. Take care of yourself and go slow. If you needed to put this book down halfway through, that's totally okay. Go at your own pace. Make a cup of tea. Embrace what serves you, and leave what doesn't. Remember that you are miraculous just for existing, and fear is not your birthright, joy is.

I hope this helps.

Warmly,

    Gracie

FURTHER READING

The Making of Biblical Womanhood: How the Subjugation of Women became Gospel Truth by Dr. Beth Allison Barr

Jesus and John Wayne: How White Evangelicals Corrupted a Faith and Fractured a Nation by Kristin Kobes Du Mez

The Great Sex Rescue: The lies you were taught and how to recover what God intended by Sheila Gregoire

Othered: Finding belonging with the God who pursues the hurt, harmed & marginalized by Jenai Auman

Women and the Gender of God : a robust theological argument against the assumption that God is Male by Amy Peeler

The Lord is my Courage: Stepping through the Shadows of Fear towards the Voice of Love by K.J. Ramsey

How to Walk into a Room: The Art of Knowing When to Stay and When to Walk Away by Emily P. Freeman

ACKNOWLEDGMENTS

In many ways, *Daughter of Breath* is the book I've been trying to write ever since I began sharing poems on the internet at seventeen years old. Back then, I entitled my blogspot blog, "You are Not Alone," and I told my parents that if my words even helped one girl realize that she wasn't the only one—and that there was healing on the other side—then it would be worth it.

A lot has happened to that seventeen year old girl since then, and writing for myself, and for that *one person*, is still my anchor sixteen years later. So before I go any further, I want to thank YOU, the Reader of this book. Thank you for reading. Thank you for making space in your heart for a shared grief—one that I wish was completely alien to you, but which I know, sadly, is not. You have endured so much, and yet, you persevere. And yet, our shredded faith perseveres—even as it changes shapes and becomes something more mysterious and nebulous than the black and white narratives of our inheritance.

You amaze me, Dear Reader. Thank you for daring to show up in this broken world, as yourself.

A huge and incomparable thank you to Bethanie Pack for yet another incredible painting that serves as the cover art of this book. Bethanie, somehow you manage to take my stilted descriptions of what I want and turn it into gorgeous artwork every time. You are incredible, and I'm so grateful to be able to continue our collaboration.

I want to thank my Spicy Dragon Ladies—especially Megan and Paige, who had to listen to an inordinate number of poems before walks and yoga sessions, and after school pickups. Thank you all for being enthusiastic readers of my early drafts, for being my constant cheerleaders, for picking me up when I fell, and for being a safe place for me to be my full self. I love you more than words can say.

Thank you to my mentor across the pond, Liezel Graham, for sharing your wisdom, experience, and kindness when this book was in its infancy, and when I'd just started coming out.

Thank you to my editors and friends Elizabeth Berget and Andi Meer for all the help fine tuning this manuscript.

Thank you to my fantastic friend, personal assistant, confidant, and "coming out coach", Sadie Seibt. You have been an anchor for me in the tossing sea of this past year, and I couldn't have done it without you. God brought you into my life at just the right time.

Thank you to my fellow writer friends, especially K.J. Ramsey and Sarah B. Southern—who believed in this book before it was even a book. Your love is ministry.

Thank you to the fabulous Jenai Auman for providing the sensitivity reading, and thank you to all my endorseres and early readers who gave me the encouragement I needed for the final leg of finishing this book.

Thank you to my parents Allan and Joy Morton, for your love, support, and commitment to a faith that is always learning and growing into the liberation that Jesus promised us.

Thank you to my daughter Ellie for her support of this "girl power" book—we've shared some sweet moments this past year around the topics of this book, and I'm so glad to have an ally like you.

Thank you to my husband Willy, for helping me with all the formatting (again) even though I used the tabs instead of indenting it properly (again). You are a life saver, and the best husband & life partner a girl could ever ask for. I treasure you.

And last, but certainly not least, thank you to my friend Jesus— we've been through some shit together, you and I. I'm so glad that through it all, I'm still yours.

ABOUT THE AUTHOR

Grace E. Kelley is a poet, personal essayist, and speculative storyteller. Across the varied genres she explores, she writes with the intent to help her readers name what aches in their own experience, so that they can move towards greater wholeness and freedom.

Daughter of Breath is her sophomore collection of poetry. Her debut collection, *as the Sparrow flies*, was released in February 2024 and is a companion for the aches of love and loss. You can find it at most major online retailers, or purchase a signed copy and other goodies at her website **gracekelleywrites.com**.

To keep up with her writing journey across the genres, be sure to check out her Personal Essay & Poetry Substack at **graceekelley. substack.com** and her Fiction Substack at **graceekelleytellmeastory. substack.com**. Or you can follow her on Instagram and Threads **@graceekelleywrites**.

NOTES

NOTES

NOTES

NOTES

NOTES

www.ingramcontent.com/pod-product-compliance
Lightning Source LLC
Chambersburg PA
CBHW060935120626
46557CB00003B/1009